75

Summary and Analysis of

THE HANDMAID'S TALE

Based on the Book
by Margaret Atwood

WORTH BOOK
SMART SUMMARIES

This Worth Books book is based on the 1994 paperback edition of *The Handmaid's Tale* by Margaret Atwood published by Virago Press.

Summary and analysis copyright © 2017 by Open Road Integrated Media, Inc.

ISBN 978-1-5040-4660-2

Worth Books
180 Maiden Lane
Suite 8A
New York, NY 10038
www.worthbooks.com

WORTH BOOKS
SMART SUMMARIES

Worth Books is a division of Open Road Integrated Media, Inc.

Contents

Context

Written in 1985, *The Handmaid's Tale* is a response to a number of cultural factors: the feminism of the 1970s, the "greed is good" zeitgeist of the 1980s, and tensions between individual liberty and exploitation (in the sex industry, for instance). Margaret Atwood says she was also inspired by the rigid religious precepts of her Puritan ancestors. The novel was regarded as a significant contribution to debate at the time and has since become a seminal work—critics and sociologists still make reference to it today. It's a simple story with a complex setting, but its simplicity packs a considerable cultural punch.

The Handmaid's Tale is a canary in the cultural coal mine, setting off warning bells that have reverberated into the early twenty-first century. The story highlights dangers that we still face and shows us what we might yet become. The fascist theocracy that it elegantly outlines remains a threat—and in some countries, such as Afghanistan, a similar government has come to power in the years after the novel was written. Atwood's book is not the first to depict a dystopian American future, but it is one of the first to illustrate how such a future might specifically impact women. Issues touched upon in the narrative, such as women's access to abortion and contraception, have continued to be relevant in the United States in the years since the book's publication.

There have been many adaptations of *The Handmaid's Tale*, including a 1990 film starring Natasha Richardson, a 2000 opera by Danish composer Poul Ruders, a 2013 Canadian ballet choreographed by Lila York, several dramatic adaptations for radio, and a television series starring Elisabeth Moss.

Overview

America has changed. War has torn the country, and nuclear power accidents along the San Andreas Fault have devastated the western seaboard. Fertility has been badly affected by pollution and disease. The president and the senate are dead, murdered by a secretive Christian theocracy that, in the ensuing chaos, takes over parts of the fragmenting nation. In what was once New England, but is now the Republic of Gilead, a repressive, shadowy government runs a state based on Biblical principles.

Offred is a Handmaid: a legalized prostitute/surrogate mother attached to the household of a powerful Commander in the new regime. The Commander's Wife, Serena Joy, is a former televangelist who cannot have children—so Offred, who is still fertile, must bear them for her. Offred's children will be considered the children of the Wife due to a ritualized impregnation ceremony that has nothing to do with sexual pleasure. The other women in the household, who are servants, look down on Offred while simultaneously hoping for her success in breeding. Meanwhile, Offred tries to block out thoughts of her husband and little daughter, lost in this brutal new nation.

Over the course of the novel we are introduced to many features of Gilead: capital punishment, the public display of the bodies of "traitors," enforced sex, torture, and, above all, a reliance on the nastier precepts of the Bible. Offred is bewildered by the transformation—how did the liberal America of her 1970s childhood come to this?

Yet, gradually, Offred's life changes. The Commander starts seeing her in private, illegally. He's a lonely man, perhaps wondering whether this fascist regime of which he was an architect is really working. Offred also begins an affair with his servant, Nick, who is a member of a secret resistance movement. And when a chance to escape presents itself, she takes it.

Does she succeed? We never fully find out, but we know of her world from a series of cassette tapes that end up in the hands of a very different culture—one that exists two hundred years later, after Gilead has collapsed and a more benign regime has emerged.

Cast of Characters

Aunt Elizabeth: A trainer at the Red Center, where women are retrained to become Handmaids. She is in charge of teaching the Handmaids about gynecology and is the one who tends to them when they are in labor.

Frederick (the Commander): An architect of the brutal regime of Gilead and a very senior official, the Commander is nonetheless a lonely and rather sad man. Although he is forbidden from seeing Offred alone, he initiates a private relationship with her. He is described as having gray hair, and Offred's doctor refers to him and his cohorts as old men.

Aunt Helena: A Red Center trainer who owned a Weight Watchers in the time before Gilead.

Janine/Ofwarren: A Handmaid from a different household who gives birth to a baby during Offred's time in the Commander's family. The women are at the Red Center at the same time, which is why Offred knows Janine's true name. While there, Janine describes being raped as a young teen, and the other women were instructed to blame her for the rape.

Luke: Offred's lost husband, seen only through her flashbacks and dreams. She doesn't know if he is alive or dead, and we never find out his fate.

Aunt Lydia: A trainer at the Red Center. Offred often remembers Aunt Lydia's advice and instructions about how to best navigate her role as a Handmaid and how she should think about the Republic of Gilead and its oppressive rules.

Moira: Offred's best friend from the time before Gilead—and a rebel under the new regime. She is confined to Jezebel's, a brothel for high-ranking officials such as the Commander. For a time, Moira was at the Red Center with Offred, but she escaped.

Nick: The Commander's chauffeur. He is willing to break small rules, such as making eye contact when he shouldn't, only buttoning up his uniform when the Commander is present, smoking cigarettes although they are a black market item. Eventually, he has an affair with Offred. Nick is an informer, but also a member of the resistance.

Offred: An American woman from a late twentieth-century liberal background, now forced to become a Handmaid for the new regime. She had a name, but it has been taken away because Handmaids are referred to by name of the man they belong to: *Offred* is "Of Fred." Offred had a husband and a daughter, both of whom have been taken from her in the new regime.

Ofglen: Another Handmaid, Offred's "twin," with whom she goes shopping. The twins are supposed to inform on each other if there is aberrant behavior, so Offred is on guard when she is with Ofglen. However, Ofglen is secretly a member of the resistance. Later, she is replaced by a different woman, who becomes "Ofglen."

Professor Pieixoto: An academic living two hundred years after Offred's time who takes her story as a historical case study. He is a professor at Cambridge University and the author of a study on Gilead and

Iran, which were both "monotheocracies" in the late twentieth century.

Serena Joy: The Commander's Wife, a former televangelist. She used to give speeches insisting that women should stay in the home, but now that her wish has come true, she is bitter and resentful of her new role.

Summary

I: Night

1

Offred is remembering the beginning—sleeping in what was once a high school gymnasium, overseen by "Aunts" who carry cattle prods and guarded by men with guns. The women, even the Aunts, are not allowed to have weapons. The men must keep their backs to the women, never looking at them.

We don't know this yet, but Offred and the other women are being retrained for service in the new state of Gilead, brutalized and persuaded into becoming obedient Handmaids rather than free women. Yet, they still rebel in small ways, mouthing their names to one another in the dead of night.

Need to Know: This is America—but not the America we know.

II: Shopping

2

Offred is in another bedroom—ostensibly a much nicer one, with pleasant furnishings—but it's still a prison. The window is shatterproof, and anything that a woman might use to hang herself has been removed. Going downstairs to the summoning sound of a bell, Offred glimpses herself in the only remaining mirror—a woman dressed in red, with red shoes and a white head covering like a nun's wimple. In the kitchen, she overhears Rita and Cora, who are Marthas, or servants. They're talking about her and how she has it easy. She could have been shipped to the Colonies, or worse.

Need to Know: The heroine is under some form of house arrest.

3

Offred goes out into the garden, which is the domain of the Commander's Wife, and she thinks about how she is not allowed to have things like gardens anymore. Offred is aware that the Wife hates her, though we don't know why yet. She recalls their first meeting, only a little over a month ago: The Wife is dressed in blue with diamonds on her finger. She is very much in a position of power over Offred. After allowing Offred to sit, she lays down the law: Offred must remember to whom the Commander belongs. Offred realizes that she recognizes the Wife from the period before Gilead. She was televangelist Serena Joy, who lobbied for a more Christian America.

Need to Know: The Commander's Wife has power over Offred but also resents her.

4

Outside, Offred sees Nick, the chauffeur, polishing the car. She'd like to speak to him, but it's too risky—perhaps he is an Eye, an informer. She meets up with Ofglen, her shopping partner. She'd like to talk to Ofglen, too, but again, it's too dangerous. So they make their way through the checkpoints to the shops in silence. This walk is part of Offred's job each day. She must purchase goods for the household and exercise her body so it remains healthy for her duties.

Need to Know: The people in the house all have different classifications. Nick, the chauffeur, is a Guardian. The men who guard the checkpoints are also Guardians, while the real soldiers are called Angels.

5

This is a part of town Offred knows. She remembers walking here with her husband, Luke, before it became Gilead. She thinks about their life before the theocracy took over—their relationship was one of equals.

She and Ofglen wait in line for produce. Many foods are rationed. A pregnant Handmaid enters, showing off her large belly—everyone envies her. Though the woman is named Ofwarren, Offred recognizes her as Janine, someone who was at the Red Center with her. None of the others at the Center had liked Janine.

Need to Know: Offred and Ofglen are stopped by a group of Japanese tourists who gawk at them. The Japanese women are dressed in the type of clothes Offred used to wear, and they are free. When the tourists wonder if the Handmaids are happy, Offred lies and says they are, because she knows the translator with them is an Eye.

6

Offred and Ofglen walk back past the church and the Wall, where the hanging corpses of dissidents are prominently displayed. On this day, the bodies are those of doctors. Offred can tell because of the white coats they wear and the placards with pictures to indicate why they were executed hanging around their necks. These men were abortionists. Offred has become somewhat desensitized to sights like this. She mostly looks at the bodies on the Wall to make sure none of them is Luke's.

Need to Know: This culture has a very visible form of capital punishment.

III: Night

7

In bed, Offred indulges herself in the only way she still can, by remembering the past. She thinks of her college friend Moira and of burning pornographic magazines at the feminist rallies her mother took her to as a child. She remembers her little daughter, too—

the girl was taken away by the state at the age of five after Offred's family's attempted escape.

Need to Know: Offred does not know what has happened to her child.

IV: Waiting Room

8

On a different day, Offred and Ofglen see new bodies on the Wall, including that of a priest. Religious dissidents are killed in Gilead—there is only room for one interpretation of Christianity here. The other corpses belonged to gay men who are identified with placards declaring that they have committed "Gender Treachery." On their walks, Offred is always aware that Ofglen might be an Eye. She must be careful to speak piously and blandly to the other woman.

Offred remembers more about Serena Joy's past as a spokesperson for this sort of oppressive theocracy; the reality of it doesn't seem to have made her happy.

Need to Know: Offred finds the Commander looking into her room, which is forbidden.

9

Since coming to this house, her second posting as a Handmaid, Offred has explored her room thoroughly. She looks for clues about its former occupant, another Handmaid. Finally, she finds a tiny message scratched into the wood of the wardrobe: *Nolite te bastardes carborundorum*. Offred doesn't know what it means, but she is comforted by this message from the past and wonders what happened to the previous Handmaid.

Need to Know: No one will tell Offred what became of the woman who last held her post.

10

Offred has more memories of Moira and the past, including Moira organizing an "underwhore" party to sell kinky underwear. It's becoming summer, and Offred thinks of how they dressed before Gilead and how different things are now. What used to seem normal has gradually changed, and now there is a new normal. She glimpses the Commander from her window—she ought to hate him, she thinks, but she doesn't.

Need to Know: Offred's best friend from college is Moira, a girl who always liked to be outrageous.

11

Offred is taken to the doctor for her regular check-up, which is a gynecological exam. She goes every month to have her fertility assessed. The doctor is male, and he offers to make her pregnant. He wants sex, which is forbidden, but he claims he's doing it to "help her out." This is both a threat and an offer—he mentions that she may be out of time soon and that older men like the Commander are probably sterile. That he would say this is shocking to Offred, not because she finds the concept surprising, but rather because the idea of men being sterile has been outlawed. It is always the woman's fault if pregnancy can't be achieved.

Offred doesn't like the idea of sex with the doctor, but she doesn't want to run the risk of offending him either. She'll think about it, she tells him.

Need to Know: If Offred doesn't get pregnant, there will be dangerous consequences for her.

12

Offred takes a bath, supervised by Cora—Handmaids are not allowed to bathe alone, in case they attempt suicide. She thinks about her lost daughter, now eight, and wonders what has become of her. Once, when her daughter was small, someone tried to steal her, which terrified Offred. Now, her daughter *has* been stolen, and Offred tries to cling to memories, but they always fade.

When Offred is given her dinner, she steals some butter, wraps it in a napkin, and hides it in her shoe.

Need to Know: Offred doesn't like to look at her body in the bath. Her entire worth in this society is her body, and she hates to be reminded of that.

V: Nap

13

While waiting for a ritual of some sort to begin, Offred sits in her room. To deal with the boredom, she remembers incidents at the training center. One of these happened during confession time: Janine, who is now the pregnant Ofwarren, confessed that she had been raped by multiple men as a young teen. The other women, led by the Aunts, jeered at her for this. Even a gang rape is the woman's fault—Janine must have led the men on. Janine's crying annoyed Offred at the time. Her weakness was unattractive.

Moira had been brought to the Red Center, too, but her spirit remained undaunted. Offred and Moira found a way to talk in the restroom so the Aunts couldn't hear them. Offred felt happier and safer with Moira there.

Need to Know: As she waits in her room, Offred remembers her daughter. They were running, being chased by men with guns. She fell, hugged her child, and tried to protect her, but they were torn apart.

VI: Household

14

Offred and the household (including the Marthas and Nick) gather in the sitting room to wait for the Commander. He's always late, and Serena Joy lets them watch the news on TV. The news is filled with unrest and crackdowns by the state, but Offred doesn't know how much of it is propaganda. African Americans are called the "Children of Ham," and the state is resettling them all in what used to be North Dakota. Dissidents shown being arrested include Quakers and Baptists.

Offred remembers her own escape attempt with Luke and her daughter. They were in their car, driving, having told their little girl they were going on a picnic.

Need to Know: The only things shown on television are religious or state-sponsored news programs. The channel broadcasting from Canada is blocked.

15

The Commander arrives and reads Biblical passages to his household, including the passage about hand-maids—surrogate wives, such as Bilhah, who bears a daughter for Rachel. The Bible is kept in a locked case because none of the women in the house are allowed to read.

Offred thinks about Moira at the Red Center. Moira tried to escape by faking illness. When she was brought back in a black van—the vehicles driven by the Eyes—her feet had been severely damaged. She'd been tortured as punishment.

Need to Know: As the Commander reads the Bible, his wife, Serena Joy, cries. She does this every time they are going to hold the upcoming ritual.

16

"The Ceremony" takes place. Offred lies on Serena Joy's bed—in fact, on Serena Joy herself. Her head rests on the Wife's stomach, and both women are fully dressed, except for Offred's undergarments. The Commander engages in intercourse with Offred as Serena Joy holds on to her hands. It's clear that this is a grim experience for everyone concerned, including the Commander. He's doing a duty, not performing an act of pleasure, as he tries to impregnate Offred as a surrogate wife. Offred wonders whether she or Serena Joy hates this more.

Need to Know: The act of sex has become a ritual devoid of joy.

17

Offred takes the stolen butter from her shoe and rubs it on her face. The Handmaids are not allowed face lotion, and this is her only option, her small rebellion. But a bigger one is to come: She sneaks downstairs, hoping to steal something (anything, just to rebel), and finds a daffodil blossom, which she takes to hide in her room for the next Handmaid. Then, to her shock, she meets Nick. He tells her that the Commander wants to see Offred alone tomorrow in his office, which is forbidden.

Need to Know: Nick and Offred kiss hungrily but pull themselves apart. The penalty for being caught together would be death.

VII: Night

18

Back in bed, Offed remembers her husband, Luke. She pictures him as a corpse, shot during their flight, or as a prisoner, or free—perhaps he managed to get to Canada after all. But these are all just imaginings. She does not know his fate.

Need to Know: The only way Offred can have hope is to believe in all the possibilities. Perhaps Luke is dead, but she believes equally that perhaps he is not. Perhaps they and their daughter will eventually be reunited.

VIII: Birth Day

19

Offred has a dream about her mother, and later that morning, as if it were an omen, a Birthmobile arrives. They all have to go to witness the birth of a baby—borne by Ofwarren (Janine). There are other Handmaids in the Birthmobile and still more at the house where Janine lives. A separate car brings all the local Wives to the same house. The atmosphere is almost party-like. The Wives are allowed alcohol.

Need to Know: Offred remembers Aunt Lydia teaching the Handmaids about childbirth. There used to be doctors and medical treatment and painkillers, which Aunt Lydia says were awful. Now women give birth naturally, with no drugs to ease the pain.

20

As Janine progresses with labor, the Wives discreetly get drunk. They are in a separate room with the Wife of the house, who is treated as if she is having the baby herself. The Handmaids all stay in the room with Janine, who is attended to by Aunt Elizabeth.

Offred remembers watching movies at the Red Center. The point of the films was to demonstrate how terrible being a woman was before the Republic of Gilead, so they showed the Handmaids old pornography and documentaries about feminists, who are now considered Unwomen. In one of the films, Offred saw her own mother, as a young woman, at a protest.

Need to Know: Offred's mother was a feminist activist who raised Offred on her own. Before, Offred found her politics too extreme. Now, she just wishes she could have everything back the way it was.

21

As Janine continues her labor, the Handmaids chant, which is supposed to help her. Indeed, some of them begin to feel as if they're in labor, too. Offred thinks they have all been drugged. Under cover of the bustling labor scene, Offred manages to speak covertly to another woman. They try to pass on information—Offred says she is looking for Moira, but the other Handmaid doesn't know Moira. She is looking for someone named Alma.

As the baby emerges, Commander Warren's Wife comes in and is seated behind Janine, as though she is the one giving birth. The baby is given a name and handed to the Wife. Janine will be allowed to breastfeed for a short time, but then she'll be reassigned. Her child belongs to Commander Warren and his Wife.

Need to Know: Offred remembers giving birth to her own baby. On the way home in the Birthmobile, she feels that all the other Handmaids are thinking of their own children as well.

22

Exhausted after the emotional day, Offred lies in her bed and thinks about Moira again. One of the main reasons that none of the Handmaids at the Red Center liked Janine was that she was an informer for the

Aunts, willing to tell them anything. Because of that, however, the Aunts gave her information sometimes. Aunt Lydia had told Moira's story to Janine, and Janine spread it to the other Handmaids.

After her first escape attempt and the subsequent punishment, Moira tried again. This time, she attacked an Aunt from behind, holding a knife to her side. Moira tied up the Aunt, took her clothes, and walked out of the Red Center as if she herself were an Aunt. None of the guards stopped her. The knife, it turned out, was actually the metal rod from one of the center's toilets. Moira was always clever.

Need to Know: After Moira's escape, the others long for news of her. She represents what is possible: the idea that they could eventually have freedom, too. But Offred has not heard anything about Moira since.

23

Offred goes to see the Commander, as he has requested. She knows it's illegal, and she is afraid. She doesn't know what to expect—but the Commander only wants her to play Scrabble with him. However, this is also forbidden for Offred, since it involves knowing how to read and write. Just to be allowed to do it feels like a small luxury. At the end of the evening, the Commander asks Offred to kiss him.

Need to Know: Offred tells the reader that this entire episode is a reconstruction of what happened, one small part of the story she will compose if she ever escapes from Gilead.

IX: Night

24

Back in her room, Offred takes stock of her life. She realizes that she needs to live in the present, work with what she's got, and not look back so much. But the effort—and the absurdity of sneaking around just to play a board game—gives her a bout of silent hysterics: She laughs and laughs, stifling the sound. If she is caught laughing, they might consider her to be unstable and take action against her. She lies on the floor, trying to compose herself.

Need to Know: Offred remembers a show she watched in her youth. The mistress of a high-ranking Nazi was interviewed and spoke of how she didn't consider the Nazi to be a monster. Offred reflects that anyone can be humanized, and it is clear she is thinking of the Commander.

X: Soul Scrolls

25

Cora finds Offred lying on the floor, where she fell asleep after her hysterics. Thinking she's dead, Cora drops the breakfast tray, terribly upset. She hints that she's seen such a thing before.

As the days pass, Offred pays more secret visits to the Commander, playing Scrabble and reading old magazines that he gives to her. He seems to like watching her as she reads.

Need to Know: In their conversations, Offred learns that the Commander holds himself to a different set of rules than those his regime imposes on others.

26

It is time for the Ceremony again, and Offred finds it increasingly awkward. The Commander is becoming more human to her, and she can no longer detach herself from the situation. Similarly, she has different feelings for Serena Joy—still hatred, but also a degree of understanding, compassion, even jealousy. And now, guilt.

Need to Know: Offred remembers Aunt Lydia telling them that the next generation of women—their daughters—will not find living this way to be as hard as they do.

27

Offred and Ofglen walk home from shopping via a route that takes them past Soul Scrolls—a chain of establishments that run automated prayer wheels. To Offred's surprise, Ofglen speaks to her without the usual pious platitudes, and it appears that Ofglen might be a member of the mysterious resistance. Ofglen has not spoken of it before, believing Offred to be genuinely pious.

Need to Know: During their walk, the Handmaids see a black van pull up. The Eyes jump out and accost a man on the street, beating him and taking him away. Everyone—even Offred—pretends not to notice. She's just relieved they didn't come for her.

28

Back home, Offred again thinks about the past—about her mother and Moira and Luke. Moira seems to have anticipated some of the unrest and, perhaps, the takeover. Offred remembers the sleazier aspects of a liberal culture as it disappeared—Pornomarts, for instance. There's the hint that this kind of excessive focus on sex produced the current backlash. She remembers losing her job and how her debit card suddenly stopped working. Luke's card continued to be in operation, and her funds had been transferred to him. All of a sudden, women were second-class citizens.

Need to Know: After the change in women's status, there were protests. Officials killed the marchers, however, and the protests quickly stopped.

29

Offred and the Commander always talk while playing Scrabble. He tells her what the message in her wardrobe means ("Don't let the bastards grind you down"), although she doesn't say where she found it. He also tells her that the previous Handmaid hanged herself because Serena Joy discovered what was going on. Offred realizes that he taught the phrase to her predecessor—she had these Scrabble sessions in the study, too. Offred asks him what she really wants to know: What's going on?

Need to Know: The Commander continues to have a relationship with Offred even though the last time he did such a thing, it led to the woman's death.

XI: Night

30

Once more, Offred is looking back, to the time of her and Luke's plans to escape. Luke offers to "take care" of their cat—they can't bring it with them, since they must pretend they are only leaving for a day trip. He kills the cat, but Offred does not ask how. She thinks of her current situation—does she really want to know what's happening? She can't recall the faces of her loved ones. She tries to pray but doesn't have a clear idea of what to pray for.

Need to Know: Offred contemplates suicide.

XII: Jezebel's

31

On one of their shopping trips, Ofglen gives Offred the resistance password: *Mayday*. When Offred gets home, Serena Joy asks her to help with winding the wool. As they complete the task, Serena Joy suggests that they use another man to impregnate Offred. In return, she gives Offred a cigarette and something much more important—the promise of a picture of Offred's daughter, who is evidently still alive.

Need to Know: Serena Joy has known all along where Offred's child is and has never told Offred.

32

Offred persuades Rita to provide her with a match, which Serena Joy gave her permission to do. However, she doesn't smoke the cigarette. Instead, she hides the match. She thinks she might be able to use it in the future, perhaps to burn down the house.

The Commander is now talking quite freely to her. Offred wants to know what is going on, and he tells her, giving her some background on the creation of Gilead. The problem was a lack of meaning among American men, everything being too easy, nothing to fight for. Gilead is better, he says, but only for some.

Need to Know: Offred imagines that the Handmaid here before her is still in the room, hanging from the chandelier. The chandelier has been removed now.

33

Ofglen and Offred attend a Prayvaganza—a group marriage ceremony—where they see Janine. She has a different partner, which means she's been transferred to a new household. Ofglen tells Offred that Janine's baby did not survive, so she was sent away.

Ofglen thinks it was Janine's own fault, because she was impregnated by a doctor, not her Commander. Offred wonders how Ofglen knows.

Need to Know: Once, at the Red Center, Janine became delusional, imagining she was back in her old life as a waitress. Moira slapped her to bring her back to reality—if they think you're crazy, they'll shoot you, Moira told Offred.

34

The Prayvaganza begins. These are arranged marriages, marrying eligible daughters to Angels, the male elite. It's much better than going through all the humiliation of high school dating, the Commander tells Offred. But Offred doesn't agree. What about love? she asks.

Need to Know: Ofglen knows Offred is seeing the Commander in private. She asks Offred to steal information for the resistance.

35

Offred can't stop thinking about the past and her lost loves. Serena Joy keeps her promise and shows Offred a photograph of her daughter, older, wearing a white dress. Offred senses that her child no longer remembers her. It's almost unbearable.

Need to Know: Offred remembers the end of her escape attempt with Luke—it was at the border, after passing several checkpoints with their faked passports, that they were finally caught.

36

The Commander gives Offred some new clothes—little more than straps and feathers—a sexy, tarty outfit. He's taking her out, he tells her, and Nick brings the car. When they pass through checkpoints, she has to crouch down and hide on the floor so that she isn't seen.

Need to Know: Offred feels strange putting on revealing clothing and makeup. It used to be normal to her, but her opinions have changed.

37

Offred recognizes the place the Commander has smuggled her into: It's a hotel she used to go to before Gilead. It is now a sex club called Jezebel's. There are women in various forms of skimpy attire all over the place. Here, Offred catches a glimpse of Moira, and her old friend sees her, too. Under the excuse of visiting the restroom, they have a chance to talk.

Need to Know: The Commander tells Offred some of the women at the sex club used to be successful businesswomen.

38

Moira tells Offred her story. After escaping from the Red Center, she made it quite a long way on the Underground Femaleroad, a system for getting women to safety. Yet, just as she and her protectors were about to board a ship for Canada, they were apprehended. She was given a choice of going to the Colonies or the sex palace, and she chose the latter. They showed her films about the Colonies, and she knew she couldn't go there. At least in Jezebel's, she gets food and a certain amount of freedom during the day. The Colonies are filled with old women and other undesirables. They are forced to clean up toxic waste, which will ultimately kill them.

Need to Know: Moira has given up on trying to escape and is resigned to life at Jezebel's. Her spirit has been broken.

39

Offred learns her mother is in the Colonies—she was in one of the films Moira was shown. It's as bad as being dead, Moira says. Offred struggles to remember the last time she saw her mother. She can't recall.

The Commander takes her to a bedroom. He wants sex, but Offred is too upset to respond the way he expects her to.

Need to Know: When Offred had realized her mother was missing, she went to her home and found signs of violence, as if she'd been taken against her will.

XIII: Night

40

Serena Joy helps Offred to sneak out and meet Nick—the obvious candidate for impregnation. Offred complies, although it's not exactly romantic. Or is it? She tells two versions of the story, leaving it to the reader to decide which, if either, is true.

Need to Know: Offred enjoys sex with Nick, but feels guilty because she doesn't know if Luke is dead.

XIV: Salvaging

41

Offred returns to Nick again and again. She's not proud of it, but it is clear that the affair is both a distraction and an escape. She wonders if the Marthas know. Her time with Nick makes her happier. She turns away from thoughts of actually escaping. Ofglen begins to lose faith in Offred and does not pass on as much information.

Need to Know: While Offred's first time with Nick was sanctioned by Serena Joy, these other meetings are strictly forbidden.

42

Offred attends a Salvaging, a euphemistic term for a public display of capital punishment in which dissidents of various kinds are hanged. Today, the doomed women are a Wife and two Handmaids. They sit on stage in front of a crowd of women who are arranged in the viewing area according to their caste—Wives and daughters in one place, Handmaids in another, etc. Aunt Lydia oversees the event. When the first Handmaid is hanged, Offred looks down. She doesn't want to watch.

Need to Know: For the first time, Aunt Lydia doesn't announce the crimes of those about to die. The audience feels cheated by this.

43

After the Salvaging comes a Particicution—an execution in which the Handmaids are allowed to participate. Aunt Lydia announces that the man is a rapist. He is torn to pieces by the assembled women. It's state-sanctioned, an outlet for their rage and hatred. Offred is surprised to see Ofglen strike the first blow, but Ofglen whispers to her that she has knocked the man out so he will not suffer as he dies—he is really a member of the resistance.

Need to Know: After the killing, Offred sees Janine, bloodstained. Janine has become delusional again and has no idea where she is or what she's done.

44

Offred goes shopping that afternoon, but, to her shock, Ofglen has changed. The new Ofglen bears the same name, but she is not the same woman. Her Commander has a new Handmaid. Offred, risking everything, tries the resistance password, but there's no sign of recognition. This Ofglen seems prim and pious, but just as they part, she whispers to Offred: Her predecessor hanged herself.

Need to Know: Ofglen killed herself because she saw a black van—the Eyes—coming for her.

45

When Offred returns from her shopping trip, Serena Joy confronts her. She has found out about the trip to Jezebel's, and she regards it as a significant betrayal. Offred doesn't know what action Serena Joy is going to take as a result.

Need to Know: Just before she is accosted by Serena Joy, Offred gives in to the fear inspired by the day's violence and danger. She will stop fighting and simply do as she's told. Finally, she has been broken.

XV: Night

46

Offred waits, numbly and in disgrace. How will Serena Joy punish her? A black van shows up to take her into custody. Knowing the Eyes will torture her, Offred wishes she had done something to fight. But it's too late now.

Nick appears first. He is an Eye, but he tells her to go with them—it's Mayday, and he calls her by her real name. So perhaps he is both an Eye and a member of the resistance. There is no way for Offred to know for sure. As she goes downstairs, she sees Serena Joy, astonished, and the Commander, who is appalled. A black-clad man tells them that she is being taken in for violation of state secrets. How could she, Serena Joy asks Offred, after all the Commander has done for her? And Offred, silent, leaves the house forever.

Need to Know: Offred knows that she is a threat to the Commander, since he has broken many rules in her presence, and she could damage him if she talks.

Historical Notes

Offred has disappeared into the mists of history, but somehow, along the way, she tapes the story we have just read, and these cassettes end up as historical artifacts at a university in the far north of Canada nearly two hundred years later. This evidence is not complete; they don't know exactly what happened to Offred or why she didn't make her story more public if she did, in fact, reach safety. However, a professor points out that she may have been trying to protect relatives still under the regime. Whatever the case,

Gilead is long gone. We should try not to judge it too harshly, says the professor.

Need to Know: Many years later, an academic conference looks back on Offred's story. Men and women seem on equal footing in this society, and they regard Gilead as an odd—and intriguing—period of history.

Character Analysis

The Commander and his Wife: Serena Joy, the Commander's Wife, is also an oppressed woman, but her fatal flaw is her early evangelism, which helped to bring this state about. She is described as a typical all-American blonde. Once a powerful televangelist, but now, with considerable irony, confined to the home in the traditional role for which she campaigned, she is bitter as a result. She might be at a higher social level than Offred, but she still scrabbles for scraps of power over the other women; she has little influence over her husband. The distinguished grey-haired Commander is ultimately undone by his hypocrisy—criticizing Radio Free America for its liberal ideas but keeping forbidden reading material at the house and patronizing the sex palace, Jezebel's. He is similar to several real-life religious leaders and represents the powerful totalitarian man who doesn't think the rules apply to him. While the Commander is highly dynamic and has a great deal of agency in his own sphere, eventually he is brought down (according to the Symposium at the end of the novel) by the constraints that the society he has engineered imposes upon him—a major irony. Both he and his Wife illustrate the fact that many people who have campaigned for dictatorial rule find themselves trapped by that rule once it comes about. They are an example of the maxim "Be careful what you wish for."

Moira and Ofglen: As foils to Offred, both Ofglen and Moira represent different choices: Moira runs and ends up in Jezebel's, taking the choice to be a state prostitute rather than be sent to the Colonies. We don't know as much about Ofglen, but she is working within the role of Handmaid, just as Offred is. However, she is more involved with the resistance, more dynamic in finding out about it than Offred (or perhaps just better placed to do so), and her way out is to commit suicide, just as the previous Offred in the Commander's household had done. The harsh reality is that it doesn't seem to matter which course a woman in Gilead takes—whether individual rebellion like Moira, organized resistance like Ofglen, or mere passive cooperation like Offred, they all remain trapped. One might look for irony in the fact that it is only the one who doesn't fight, Offred, who ultimately escapes. But Offred's escape is mostly a matter of luck, arranged for her by others, and even then, we are not sure she reaches freedom.

Offred: Our heroine, Offred, has many antagonists, including the elite of Gilead, the Eyes, the Commander and his Wife, and the other oppressed women who surround her. Under a totalitarian regime, she can trust no one and is constantly looking back to her happier past. She reflects on her passivity and lack of agency, but in the reality of the novel, she has little choice: Direct rebellion will get her killed. Even tiny acts of defiance, such as being caught reading, could result in harsh punishment. She knows that her husband, Luke, was shot during their escape attempt, but she doesn't know whether or not he died. Her daughter was taken away from her and given to an unknown family to be raised in the way the theocracy wants—taught to be subservient and silent, she will not even learn to read.

Atwood shows us how people under extreme pressure will take any bit of power as a kind of compromise, but they don't really have any control. So Offred will risk sleeping with Nick because it gives her a tiny moment of freedom. It is still not control over her destiny, however. In fact, when she flees, it's because Nick engineered it. Even the Commander, who is not unkind to her, treats her as a piece of property. Her direct antagonist is Serena Joy, who, apart from the Commander and the state itself, has the most power over her and who dislikes and resents her presence. The situation is too serious for any character to play the role of a comic foil: There is humor here, but it is extremely bleak and mainly takes the form of irony. We may regard Nick—a secret member of the resistance but also an informing Eye—as anti-heroic. He's an ambivalent character, and because his motivations are hidden from Offred, they're concealed from us as well.

Despite all this, Offred is very strong. She detaches herself from her circumstances to some degree, holding on to the past as her anchor. She contemplates suicide briefly, but does not act on those thoughts. Naturally, much of her internal reflection is devoted to her lost loved ones, and although she finds out a little about what has happened to them, she can never be certain. This is a terrible situation for anyone to be in, and Offred deals with it as best she can, though she gives way to anguish sometimes. She knows that she has to try to live her life in the present and not look back, but, of course, this is almost impossible. As a female character, she exemplifies the plight of the ordinary woman caught up in events beyond her control. In the context of this narrative, Offred is "everywoman"—not a superheroine, merely someone trying to get by in a dangerous world. Other women, like Moira and Ofglen, take bigger risks, but it depends on personal circumstances to some degree, because Offred has to think of her daughter, her mother, and Luke. If they're still alive, she's reluctant to do anything to jeopardize their situations. Because Offred is narrating the story, and does not need to dwell on her own physical characteristics, we don't know much about what she looks like—she is rendered even more invisible, just as the state would like her to be.

Professor Pieixoto and Professor Crescent Moon:
These academics, who run the conference held centuries in the future, are merely stand-ins to provide us with a historical view of Gilead. Nevertheless, the easy banter and camaraderie between the pair demonstrates the stark contrast between Offred's society and their own. A man and a woman, they are on equal footing as scholars and treat each other with respect. The society in which the conference appears is very different from Gilead, and though the proceedings are formal and quite brief, we learn a lot from them: Women are allowed to read; life is not only about work, but also about having fun; and the state of Gilead is long dead and an object of study rather than of hatred and fear. The academics find parts of Offred's story almost

amusing—but, ironically, although her tale is now taking center stage, she's still being treated as property: a historical curiosity rather than a real person.

Themes and Symbols

Eyes: Eyes appear frequently in this novel, including the all-seeing eye of the state and its spies and the eye that is painted on the cars of the elite's Guardians. Offred is watched all the time—she even has an eye tattooed on her ankle to remind her of it. She suspects that Nick is an Eye, and she is right, but he is an Eye for both the state and the resistance, an eye that looks both ways. While the eye acts as a symbol of oppression, ultimately, Offred herself becomes an eye: She is the silent observer who reveals the workings of Gilead to those who come later.

Flowers: Flowers appear throughout the book as examples of the natural world that even Gilead can't completely control and as symbols of beauty and freedom. The Commander's Wife spends a great deal of time in her garden—perhaps her moments of freedom from the oppressiveness of the household, a structure for which she campaigned. Offred steals a daffodil to conceal in her room as a message for the next Handmaid; a flower is thus a part of her own small rebellion against Gilead.

Religion: Although God and godliness are constant themes in Gilead, there is little sense that the people involved in the story have any real faith. Offred notices that Bible passages have been changed to suit the needs of the state. Prayer has been outsourced to the Soul Scrolls store. Piousness is an act put on by the Commander, who engages in immoral behavior in private with no apparent sense of guilt. Offred doesn't reject the idea of God—she notes, however, that this society isn't what the actual God would want.

Use of color: Color is used as means of symbolism throughout the novel. The red assigned to Handmaids serves a dual purpose: Red for blood, like menstrual blood, symbolizing fertility; scarlet to symbolize fallen women. Blue is for the Wives—it is the color of the Virgin Mary's dress, symbolizing the purity, goodness, and power that the Wives are supposed to hold. Green is for the Marthas, the servants. Finally, the Econowives wear striped garments, symbolizing their multi-role status. Interestingly, this use of color is employed both by Atwood as the author and by Gilead itself. Professor Pieixoto explains that one of the men, who was possibly Offred's Commander, had a background in marketing and consciously chose to dress women in specific uniforms and colors.

Women's bodies: To use an old slogan, in Gilead, the "personal is political." Women's bodies are politicized and made into tools: No one escapes being an instrument of the state, whether as a breeding woman, a servant, or even a Wife. Women are defined by their gender roles, and sometimes even their names are taken away from them—Handmaids are referred to solely by the names of the men to whom they belong. Since the creation of Gilead was partially a response to a crisis in fertility, the state has reduced women to nothing more than vehicles of procreation. This is Atwood taking the idea of government control over women's reproductive choices to its extreme conclusion.

Women's relationships: A consistent theme is how women support, but also betray, one another. Examples of support include Ofglen giving Offred the resistance password and Moira and Offred exchanging information at Jezebel's—these are women bonding together against oppression. However, there are also examples of women acting against one another: the support that Serena Joy originally gives to Gilead, Janine's work as an informer at the Red Center, and the assignment of partners/spies for each Handmaid.

Direct Quotes and Analysis

"Ordinary, said Aunt Lydia, is what you are used to. This may not seem ordinary to you now, but after a time it will. It will become ordinary."

The Handmaids are retrained by the state, so what would once have been appalling now becomes normal. In order to change society, the values and behaviors of the people must be modified; to make the Handmaids accept their new role as property, their expectations are radically altered from the previous norm of being autonomous citizens. While before, such a thing as a Particicution would have been utterly unthinkable, the normalization of corporal punishment has made the act seem ordinary and acceptable. On a more personal level, the Ceremony, which in the past would have been seen as rape, is now considered to be merely duty to the state and to God.

"She doesn't make speeches anymore. She has become speechless. She stays in her home, but it doesn't seem to agree with her. How furious she must be, now that she has been taken at her word."

The Commander's Wife, Serena Joy, was once a televangelist, preaching that women should be confined to the home—as she is now. The irony is that she chafes under the restriction and misses her old power. There is a real-life analogy in the Westboro Baptist Church, which decided that its matriarchal spokeswoman had too much power and transferred her duties to an all-male committee. Offred's wry observation that Serena Joy brought this on herself is an example of the dark humor that occasionally punctuates this bleak story.

"Don't let the bastards grind you down."

This is the phrase that Offred finds carved into her wardrobe in "dog Latin." She knows that the previous Handmaid has put it there as a message to her, and it comforts her even before she knows what it means. It turns out to be a quote that the Commander had taught her predecessor. Knowing this, Offred realizes that he'd had an illicit relationship with that Offred, too—a relationship that led to the woman committing suicide. It is a sad irony that the Handmaid who had left such a message of strength ultimately wasn't able to stay strong in the end.

"We were the people who were not in the papers. We lived in the blank white spaces at the edges of print. It gave us more freedom. We lived in the gaps between the stories."

Here, Offred is referring to the lives of regular people in the time before Gilead. It is a standard human reaction: While you may read news stories about people treating one another horribly, the typical response is to feel that such things can't happen to you. This is Offred's explanation of that phenomenon. In *The Handmaid's Tale*, there is a secondary meaning: The Handmaids are literally marginalia. They're sidelined from everything except childbearing, and once they're too old for that, they are discarded.

"Better never means better for everyone. . . . It always means worse, for some."

This is the Commander's justification for the existence of Gilead when Offred raises the thorny question as to why it is such an awful society for women.

Like so many dictatorships, the elite of Gilead believe that they caused change for the public good—no matter how many people suffer as a result.

Trivia

1. Offred's real name may be June. The clue is in the list of names that the women whisper to one another in Chapter 1.

2. The academic conference in 2195 is held in the Arctic Circle, in Denay, Nunavit—which, when read out loud, is pronounced like "Deny None of It."

3. Offred finds a desk with graffiti carved into it: "M. loves G. 1972." Margaret Atwood has been with her partner, Graeme Gibson, since the early 1970s.

4. In America around 1980, evangelicals such as Tim LaHaye were saying that God didn't intend for America to be a democracy, but rather a theocratic dictatorship.

5. *The Handmaid's Tale* was made into an opera with music by Poul Ruders.

6. Margaret Atwood invented a long-distance pen, which enables her to sign fans' books while not in the same location.

7. *The Handmaid's Tale* was adapted into a Hulu series released in 2017. The series stars Joseph Fiennes as the Commander and Elisabeth Moss as Offred.

8. The novel is dedicated to Mary Webster, an ancestor of Atwood's who was hanged as a witch but survived her hanging.

9. When asked by a fan on Twitter, "[W]hy do we never get to know [O]ffred's real name?" Margaret Atwood replied, "Many reasons . . . so many people have been re-named over the centuries, their original names [are] lost. That was my thought at the time."

10. *The Handmaid's Tale* frequently appears on "banned books" lists, which some may find ironic, given that it features a totalitarian society in which women are not allowed to read.

What's That Word?

Angels: Soldiers for the Republic of Gilead.

Aunts: Women whose role is to train—and police—other women.

Children of Ham: The African American population being relocated to remote areas.

Colonies: A euphemism for work camps. The Colonies are areas of toxic waste that must be cleaned, and those who are sent there are used as laborers until they die, poisoned by the environment.

Econowife: A woman whose role is that of wife to a

lower-class man; such women play all the female roles which are performed separately by Marthas, Wives, and Handmaids in wealthier homes.

Eye: An informer for the state; a spy.

Handmaid: A woman whose only function is breeding children.

Jezebels: Prostitutes; many Jezebels were professional women in their pre-Gilead lives.

Keepers: Babies who are viable.

Martha: A woman whose role is that of a household servant.

Prayvaganza: A mass marriage ceremony for eligible girls or a mass celebration for male veterans returning from the war. Attendance is segregated by gender.

Salvaging: A capital punishment ceremony. Again, attendance—and execution—is segregated by gender.

Sons of Jacob: The Jewish population forced to choose between converting or being relocated to Israel.

Unbabies/shredders: Babies who are not viable.

Unwomen: Women who can't be put into Gilead's hierarchy: feminists, nuns, sterile women, political dissidents, and lesbians. Unwomen are sent to the Colonies.

Critical Response

- Arthur C. Clarke Award
- Booker Prize finalist
- Governer General's Award for English Language Fiction
- Nebula Award finalist
- Prometheus Award

"Just as the world of Orwell's *1984* gripped our imaginations, so will the world of Atwood's handmaid. . . . *The Handmaid's Tale* is a novel that brilliantly illuminates some of the darker interconnections between politics and sex."   —*The Washington Post*

"*The Handmaid's Tale* deserves the highest praise."
—*San Francisco Chronicle*

"Atwood takes many trends which exist today and stretches them to their logical and chilling conclusions. . . . An excellent novel about the directions our lives are taking. . . . Read it while it's still allowed."
—*Houston Chronicle*

About
Margaret
Atwood

Margaret Atwood was born in 1939 in Ottowa and was brought up in Ontario, Quebec, and Toronto. Educated at the University of Toronto and Radcliffe College, she has worked extensively as a university lecturer and writer, publishing more than forty works of fiction, critical essays, and poetry. Her fiction includes both novels and short stories.

Atwood's novels have earned the highest accolades, with *The Blind Assassin* winning the Booker Prize and *Alias Grace* winning both the Giller Prize in Canada and the Premio Mondello in Italy. She draws on feminist and historical issues, often using the tropes of science fiction, although she has denied that she should be categorized as a science fiction writer. She draws a distinction between speculative fiction, of which *The Handmaid's Tale* is an example, and science fiction.

Atwood was President of the Writers' Union of Canada from May 1981–May 1982 and was President of International P.E.N. Canadian Center (English Speaking) from 1984–1986. She lives in Toronto with her partner, Graeme Gibson.

For Your Information

Online

"Book Review." NYTimes.com

"*The Handmaid's Tale* Cast and Creators Think Margaret Atwood's Story Is Always Relevant." Nerdist.com

"*The Handmaid's Tale*: A Warning About Patriarchy and Power." EarlyBirdBooks.com

"Haunted by The Handmaid's Tale." TheGuardian.com

"Offred's Complicity and the Dystopian Tradition in Margaret Atwood's *The Handmaid's Tale*." Journals.Lib.UNB.ca

"Puns, Puzzles and Easter Eggs in Margaret Atwood's *The Handmaid's Tale*." Gizmodo.com

"What Choice Would You Make?: Margaret Atwood
& Steve Paulson Discuss Dystopias, Prostibots &
Hope." EelectricLiterature.com

Books
The Fifth Sacred Thing by Starhawk
The Gate to Women's Country by Sheri S. Tepper
Margaret Atwood and the Labour of Literary Celebrity
by Lorraine York
Walk to The End of the World by Suzy McKee Charnas

Other Books by Margaret Atwood
Alias Grace
The Blind Assassin
Cat's Eye
The Edible Woman
Hag-Seed
The Heart Goes Last
Lady Oracle
MaddAddam
Negotiating with the Dead: A Writer on Writing
Oryx and Crake
The Penelopiad
The Robber Bride
Stone Mattress
Surfacing
The Tent
The Year of the Flood

Bibliography

Abrahams, Daniel. "Puns, Puzzles and Easter Eggs in Margaret Atwood's *The Handmaid's Tale*." Gizmodo, 2011.

Atwood, Margaret. *The Handmaid's Tale*. Toronto, McLelland and Stewart, 1985.

McCarthy, Mary. "Book Review." *The New York Times*. February 9, 1986.

Weiss, Allen. "Offred's Complicity and the Dystopian Tradition in Margaret Atwood's *The Handmaid's Tale*." *Studies in Canadian Literature/Études en literature canadienne*. York University, 2009.

WORTH BOOKS
SMART SUMMARIES

So much to read,
so little time?

Explore summaries of bestselling
fiction and essential nonfiction
books on a variety of subjects,
including business, history, science,
lifestyle, and much more.

Visit the store at
www.ebookstore.worthbooks.com

MORE SMART SUMMARIES
FROM WORTH BOOKS

CLASSIC FICTION

WORTH BOOKS
SMART SUMMARIES

MORE SMART SUMMARIES
FROM WORTH BOOKS

EMPOWERMENT

WORTH BOOKS
SMART SUMMARIES

MORE SMART SUMMARIES
FROM WORTH BOOKS

TRENDING

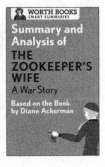

WORTH BOOKS
SMART SUMMARIES